SUGGESTIONS FOR GROUP LEADERS

1 THE ROOM
Discourage people from sitting outside or behind the main circle. All need to be equally involved.

2. HOSPITALITY
Tea or coffee on arrival can be helpful at the first meeting. Perhaps at the end too, to encourage folk to talk informally. Some groups might be more ambitious, taking it in turns to bring a dessert to start the evening (even in Lent, hospitality is ok!) with coffee at the end.

3. THE START
If group members do not know each other well, some kind of 'icebreaker' might be helpful. You might invite people to share something quite secular (where they grew up, holidays, hobbies, significant object, etc.) or something more 'spiritual' (one thing I like and one thing I dislike about my church/denomination). Place a time limit on this.

4. PREPARING THE GROUP
Take the group into your confidence, e.g. 'I've never done this before' or 'I've led lots of groups and every one has contained surprises'. Sharing vulnerability is designed to encourage all members to see the success of the group as their responsibility. Encourage those who know that they talk easily, to ration their contributions. You might introduce a fun element by producing a bell which all must obey instantly. Encourage the reticent to speak at least once or twice – however briefly. Explain that there are no 'right' answers and that among friends it's fine to say things that you are not sure about – to express half-formed ideas. But of course, if individuals choose to say nothing, that is alright too.

5. THE MATERIAL
Encourage members to read next week's chapter before the meeting, if possible. Don't attempt to answer all questions – a lively exchange of views is what matters. If you wish to spread a session over two or more meetings, that's fine.

You might decide to play all or part of the cassette at the end as well as the beginning. If you decide to use an extract, you are advised to use a different copy of the cassette from that used at the beginning. Get it ready at the precise point – finding a specific place can be difficult, especially when others are watching!

For some questions you might start with a few minutes' silence to make jottings. Or you might ask members to talk in sub-groups of two or three, before sharing with the whole group.

6. PREPARATION
Decide beforehand whether to distribute (or ask people to bring) paper, pencils, Bibles, hymn books etc. If possible, ask people in advance to read a passage or lead in prayer, so that they can prepare.

7. TIMING
Try to start on time and make sure you stick fairly closely to your stated finishing time.

SESSION 1:
FAITH FACING FACTS

Stuart Blanch, Archbishop of York from 1975 to 1983, wrote a book entitled *Living By Faith*. One striking point which he made was that every single person is a believer. There is no opting out.

Some of my atheist friends like to think that they sit in a spectators' gallery. From this vantage point they look with puzzled interest on those of us who live by faith, while they live by logic and certainty.

This is nonsense, of course. Christians *believe* that God exists and that God is love. Atheists *believe* that there is no God, and the world has no purpose. Agnostics *believe* that there is insufficient evidence to decide either way. Those who are indifferent *believe* that these questions are unimportant.

The question is not, 'Are you a believer?' but, 'What do you believe in?', and 'Is your faith based on good reasons?'

Christians delight to be called 'believers' because we put our faith in Jesus Christ. What are the facts that enable us to make this act of faith with integrity? From a list of possibilities, I select three:

1. The fact of Jesus Christ*

In 1913 the Cambridge mathematician G.H. Hardy 'discovered' a brilliant Indian mathematician called Srinivasa Ramanujan. It happened like this...

Ramanujan – an Indian clerk with little formal education – wrote a long letter to Hardy which was full of complicated mathematical formulae. This posed a puzzle for Hardy: was the letter a hoax or was it genuine? Hardy soon realised that even his cleverest students could not have invented the letter; the mathematics were far too advanced and original.

He remarked: 'I had never seen anything in the least like them before. A single look at them was enough to show that they could only be written down by a mathematician of the highest class... they must be true

---

*Note: *The Fact of Jesus Christ* is taken from *Live Your Faith*, also available from York Courses

because, if they were not true, no-one would have the imagination to invent them.'

'They must be true because, if they were not true, no-one would have the imagination to invent them.' It seems to me that the same can be said of much of the material in the New Testament – and especially those claims made for and by Jesus. They simply must be true, because no-one would have had the imagination to invent them – least of all *Jewish* men and women to whom they would have been so shocking. You would need someone of the stature of Jesus to invent the teaching of Jesus.

2. *The fact of transformation*

Malcolm Worsley was a thief. He was well known to the police and often caught. As he left prison yet again, a prison officer commented, 'You'll be back Worsley.' This stung Malcolm, but the officer was right. Malcolm *did* go back – not as a prisoner, but as a probation officer. For in his heart, Malcolm had heard the voice of Jesus Christ saying, 'Follow me.' He accepted that invitation. Since then Malcolm has worked with drug addicts and others in need. In July 1996 he was ordained as a minister in the Church of England.

Dramatic conversions like this have taken place since the time of Saul of Tarsus. Saul, a committed persecutor of the Christian church, was famously transformed into St. Paul, the apostle to the nations. There is a single factor which links such dramatic conversions across the centuries. This is the conviction by those transformed that they have encountered the risen Christ. They claim that he is at the centre of their lives – bringing guidance, inspiration and challenge.

3. *The fact of widespread experience*

Most Christians do not come to faith by such dramatic means. Many of us became believers through a long process in which we met Church members who encouraged, impressed, and sometimes inspired us, by their integrity, love, and down-to-earth goodness.

Those Christians – the majority – who do not have a dramatic story to tell, do have *some* experience of the risen Christ. Many have a sense of being 'accompanied' through life by an unseen presence who encourages, directs, inspires, renews and challenges them. They identify this presence as the Risen Lord.

The above three facts do not exhaust the evidence by any means. But taken together they are – in my view at least – impressive testimony to the Christian claim that Jesus Christ is alive and active in our world today.

'I am absolutely convinced that at the heart of the Christian story is an historical event. I'm as convinced as it's possible to be, that God has acted within human history in Jesus, whose life is well enough attested for me to feel that it is factual. I'm not going to waste my time arguing about the factuality of this detail or that detail, because I know that at the centre of it all, God – the transcendent Other – has entered human history and has found a way (He has found a way!) of entering the life that I live... I don't have to explain it; I have to experience it.'

(Dr Leslie Griffiths on the audio-tape which accompanies this booklet)

QUESTIONS FOR GROUPS

Please read page 1 (especially paragraphs 4 & 5) before the discussion starts. Some groups will not have time to attempt more than a few questions. That is fine; this is not an obstacle course!

Suggested Bible Reading: Luke 1:1-4

1. Raise any points on the audio tape or in the booklet with which you strongly agree or disagree.

2. How did you come to faith in Jesus Christ? What key points would you select e.g. particular experiences, meetings, people, organisations, church activities...? You may want to spend time on this and question each other.

3. What would you say to an atheist friend who accused you of living by superstition, while she lived by logic?

4. What would you say to a friend who was 'into' horoscopes and assumed that his faith and yours were very similar?

5. Are the three facts outlined in Chapter 1 important for your faith? Why or why not?

6. What other facts encourage, inform or challenge your faith?

*7. Do you know anyone who has had a dramatic conversion experience? Have you?

*8. Do you share a sense of being 'accompanied' through life by the risen Christ? Can you describe this to other group members?

9. Does your faith in God give you strength for life in the twenty-first century? Can you give examples?

10. Read Acts 1:1-8 What are the key facts which Luke, the author of Acts, seeks to establish? What was their significance for him and what is their significance for us?

SESSION 2:
FAITH FACING DOUBT

In today's church, doubt is sometimes regarded as a virtue. In many churches, members are encouraged to voice doubts and difficulties (in Lent groups, for example!). This is almost all gain, for it makes for an atmosphere of honesty and openness. We don't need to pretend to one another.

It remains true that doubt is not given a good press in the Bible. Clearly there is a tension here. Why is doubt condemned in the scriptures? I suggest this is because our relationship with God is deeply personal – and 'good faith' between people is essential if a relationship is to flourish. Nothing puts a human relationship under greater threat than the words, 'I don't trust you'. The same is true of our relationship with God.

But the God of the Bible dislikes pretence even more than he dislikes doubt. He wants us to be honest as we express our deepest emotions, fears and hopes in prayer. 'Lord I believe; help my unbelief' is a statement which Jesus understands (see Mark 9:24).

Various factors need to be taken into account when we consider religious doubt. These include:

- *Personality.* Some people seem to be born optimists; others are much more pessimistic or lugubrious. The former see the glass as half full; the latter see it as half empty. To some extent our ability to trust, and the nature of our doubts, are related to our personalities.

- *Experience of the world.* If, as children, we are badly let down by the adults around us, then trust becomes much more difficult. Doubt becomes a way of life which we adopt to guard against deep hurt.

Doubt takes two forms. The first is *fundamental doubt.* This is experienced by those Christians who sometimes wonder whether Christianity is a complete fiction. I know an outstanding Christian leader who is plagued in this way. 'I am a long term sufferer from serious doubt', he comments. 'But doubt does not mean that God is not there. I just plough on and follow Christ as though the whole thing *is* true.'

Many Christians experience fundamental doubt from time to time, especially when confronted by personal disaster, or calamity on a vast scale. Interestingly though, personal suffering often *strengthens* faith. It is those who stand by and observe the suffering of others who find their faith most severely challenged.

The other kind of doubt relates to particular items in the Christian Creeds. Some believers accept all aspects of the Christian faith without difficulty and with few questions. Others accept the central core of Christianity while struggling with particular aspects of traditional Christian teaching – the reality of hell perhaps, or the Virgin Birth, or the Ascension into heaven, or...

The most famous of all doubters is St. Thomas. From his experience we learn that wrestling with doubt can strengthen faith. Dr. George Carey, Archbishop of Canterbury, put it like this: 'Doubt has stirred me to greater faith.' A Polish proverb states this even more strongly: 'To believe with certainty we must begin with doubting.'

But we should not emphasise the *mental* aspects of faith and doubt too strongly. In the Bible, faith is not just a question of holding particular beliefs. Faith informs our attitudes, our approach to life and our actions.

The acid test of true faith is not whether we can put ticks against a checklist of statements in the Creeds. The most important test is whether we truly follow Jesus Christ as his disciples. What really matters is whether the fruit of the Spirit grows in our lives (see Galations 5:22) and whether we show our faith by our stewardship, our commitment, our sacrifice and our love. If we fail to exhibit adventurous faith it may be that we are atheists *in practice,* however orthodox we may be in our heads. As the apostle Paul put it, 'The only thing that counts is faith expressing itself through love.' (Galatians 5:6)

'Not only does a Christian believe; he is a person who 'thinks in believing and believes in thinking', as Augustine expressed it. The world of Christian faith is not a fairy-tale, make-believe world, question-free and problem-proof, but a world where doubt is never far from faith's shoulder... If ours is an examined faith, we should be unafraid to doubt. If doubt is eventually justified, we were believing what clearly was not worth believing. But if doubt is answered, our faith has grown stronger still. It knows God more certainly and it can enjoy God more deeply'.

(*Doubt* by Os Guinness, Lion Publishing)

QUESTIONS FOR GROUPS

Suggested Bible Reading: Psalm 13

1. Raise any points on the audio tape or in the bookle with which you strongly agree or disagree.

2. Do you sometimes experience fundamental doubt, o do you know others who do? Describe and explai this. Do you find it difficult to be completely open an honest about your inner feelings? Is it wise to wear ou hearts on our sleeves?

3. Some modern Christians seem almost ashamed at no experiencing doubt, because they might be thought t be shallow. Ann Widdecombe criticises this approac and affirms a sense of certainty. Where do you stan on this?

4. Are there any particular aspects of the Christian fait which you find difficult to believe?

5. The great Archbishop William Temple experienced fev doubts. This had one drawback. He felt that this mad evangelism more difficult because he found it hard t empathise with doubters and sceptics. What do yo think about this?

6. In Luke 24:41 we read that the disciples 'disbelieve for joy'. News of the resurrection simply seemed to good to be true. What do you make of that?

7. In the depths of his terrible trials, Job declarec 'Though he slay me, yet will I trust Him' (Job 13:15). that blind faith or heroic faith? Could Job be accuse of self-deception?

8. What are the main factors which trigger doubt in th twenty first century and how might we approach an tackle these?

9. In his summary the Archbishop suggests that for all hi apparent doubts, Steve Chalke isn't *really* a doubte because he gets on with the all-important business c costly, involved discipleship. Are you happy with thi viewpoint? Re-read the paragraph before the bo (page 7) before discussing this.

10. Read 2 Corinthians 1:1-11. Paul is not sentiment about suffering – his own experiences forced him to b realistic. But he does suggest that good can come fro suffering. What is his teaching on this, and how can w apply it today?

SESSION 3:
FAITH FACING DISASTER

Two years before he died, I had the great privilege of interviewing Lord Tonypandy – better known as George Thomas MP, Speaker of the House of Commons from 1976 to 1983.

George was Secretary of State for Wales during the terrible disaster in Aberfan in 1966. A huge slide of coal dust engulfed the village and 144 people were killed, including many children. When asked how this affected his faith, George responded that he didn't blame God for the disaster – he blamed the National Coal Board.

Many disasters are man-made. True, the climate is sometimes hostile, producing drought, flood and famine. But most nations are able to survive these catastrophes, if they are well-governed and living in peace. It is poor governments and wars that turn these natural calamities into large-scale human disasters.

But of course, this does not remove the difficulty. The problem of innocent suffering is *the greatest* problem for those of us who believe that God is love. Why do such disasters happen? Why doesn't God step in to prevent them? Such questions have troubled Christians and provided ammunition for our critics, for many a century. In these days of mass communication we are even more acutely aware of calamities. We live in a 'global village'; disasters from all over the world are brought into our homes via the television screen.

There are no glib, easy, answers to the deep question of innocent suffering, but there are at least two points which need to be made.

1. The way the world is

John Polkinghorne, former Professor of Mathematical Physics at Cambridge University, put it like this:*

'God does not bring about everything that happens in the world. Because God is a God of love, he allows creatures to be themselves and to make themselves. That sort of valuable, worthwhile, independent creation has a

---

*In Science and Christian Faith, a 60 minute conversation on audio-tape with John Young (available from York Courses).

9

cost. We see that in the terrible cruel choices of humankind. We also see it in the physical history of the world. Exactly the same bio-chemical processes that enable some cells to mutate and produce new forms of life – the very engine that has driven the amazingly fruitful history of life here on earth – will allow other cells to mutate and to become malignant.

You just cannot have one without the other. The tragic fact that there is cancer in the world is not because God did not bother – it is a necessary cost of a world allowed to make itself'.

2.   *The death of Jesus*   .

Christians have always believed that, in a profound way, the cross of Christ provides a key to the pressing question of innocent suffering.

To put this simply and personally, I recall a conversation with a mother whose young child had just died. She told me that she drew great comfort from one particular Bible verse. 'Which verse is that?' I asked, expecting her to speak of resurrection and the life of heaven. To my surprise she took me to the desolate words of Jesus from the cross, where he quoted from Psalm 22: 'My God, my God, why have you forsaken me?' She felt that Jesus understood her sense of despair and desolation, because he had been there too.

All Christians draw comfort from the belief that their Saviour has immersed himself in the bitter pains of a suffering world. He does not stand aloof, but understands 'from the inside'.

One of the great Chaplains of the First World War was G.A. Studdert-Kennedy (known as Woodbine Willie) He recorded these words in his diary.

'On June 7th , 1917, I was running to our lines half mad with fright... being heavily shelled. As I ran I stumbled and fell over something. It was an undersized, underfed German boy, with a wound in his stomach and a hole in his head.... Then there came light.... It seemed to me that the boy disappeared and in his place there lay the Christ

upon his cross, and cried, 'Inasmuch as ye have done it unto the least of these my little ones ye have done it unto me.' From that moment on I never saw a battlefield as anything but a crucifix. From that moment on I have never seen the world as anything but a crucifix.'

One of the central Christian claims is that, in some deeply mysterious sense, Jesus died for us. This carries a great challenge because, in turn, he calls us to 'die' with him ('Take up your cross, deny yourself, and follow me'). Equally important is the glorious truth that he died, not only *for us*, but *with us* – alongside us, sharing our suffering and pain.

We are not on our own in a cold, uncaring universe. At the heart of all things we do not find indifference; we find costly love and compassion. The evidence for this is to be found at Golgotha, outside a city wall. And in a garden with an empty tomb.

> 'I could never myself believe in God if it were not for the cross. In the real world of pain, how could one worship a God who was immune from it'
> (*The Cross of Christ* by John Stott, IVP)

QUESTIONS FOR GROUPS

Suggested Bible Reading: Romans 5:1-5

1. Raise any points on the audio tape or in the booklet with which you strongly agree or disagree.

2. Have you experienced personal tragedy, or do you know people who have? What did this do to your/their faith?

3. I wrote these questions in my garden and noticed a dead mouse near my chair. Clearly it had been killed by a cat. Everyday occurrences like this disturb my faith. Am I being sentimental?

4. What do you make of the quotation from Professor John Polkinghorne in this chapter? Do you find it helpful?

5. Do you understand the attitude and comments of the bereaved mother in this chapter, and how do you feel about the comments of Woodbine Willie and John Stott?

6. Re-read the paragraph above the quotation from John Stott in the Box (page 11). Do you feel the force of this? Where else is the evidence to be found?

7. Death is often viewed as the ultimate disaster but the New Testament does not agree. Does the hope heaven help as you contemplate:

   (a) large-scale disasters?

   (b) your own mortality?

8. As you contemplate the ultimate 'disaster' of death have you made practical plans e.g. have you made will and planned your own funeral service? Are such steps helpful or depressing, in your view?

9. Steve Chalke experienced a strong fear of death as a child. His faith has helped him overcome this, although he fears the process of dying.

   (a) How do you relate to that?

   (b) Do most young people ponder death? Or are such musings found mainly among older people, in your experience?

10. Read Acts 8:1-2 and 1 Peter 1:3-9

    (a) What are the main points which emerge in the passages?

    (b) How can they help us in our day-to-day lives?

    (c) Can you select one short phrase to memorise and treasure?

A few years ago I saved the entire world from disaster. It happened like this... A woman from our local psychiatric hospital called and warned me that a terrible catastrophe was about to engulf the planet. I suggested that we should go into church and pray that God would prevent this. She readily agreed and we knelt together and prayed. The fact that you are reading this short chapter proves that prayer works.

If only it were that simple!

Does prayer work? Does praying make a difference? If we pray and the desired outcome occurs, there are always two possible explanations. Yes, our prayers made all the difference or No, it would have happened anyway. To 'read' the situation in the first way requires an act of faith. To read the situation in the second way requires an act of scepticism. Witnesses can be found on either side of the argument.

Mark Twain's Huckleberry Finn was clear that prayer is a waste of time:

> 'Miss Watson she took me in the closet and prayed, but nothing come of it. She told me to pray every day, and whatever I asked for I would get it. But it warn't so. I tried it. Once I got a fish-line, but no hooks. It warn't any good to me without hooks. I tried for the hooks three or four times, but somehow I couldn't make it work. I set down, one time, back in the woods, and had a long think about it. I says to myself, if a body can get anything they pray for, why don't Deacon Winn get back the money he lost on pork? Why can't the widow get back her silver snuffbox that was stole? Why can't Miss Watson fat up? No, says I to myself, there ain't nothing in it.'

In contrast, the Russian poet Irina Ratushinskaya testifies powerfully to the power of intercessory prayer. Irina spent four years in Soviet labour camps for her literary and human-rights activities.

In one of her poems, Irina describes herself as 'a huddle by an icy wall' This gives a harrowing picture of the biting cold, the inadequate clothing and the poor diet in those terrible camps. But she testifies to two kinds

of warmth which she sometimes experienced: the inner
emotional warmth of joy, and a physical warmth
throughout her body, despite the freezing conditions. It
is her conviction that these phenomena (experienced
by other prisoners, too) were a direct answer to prayer

> *Believe me, it was often thus*
> *In solitary cells, on winter nights*
> *A sudden sense of joy and warmth*
> *And a resounding note of love.*
> *And then, unsleeping, I would know*
> *A huddle by an icy wall:*
> *Someone is thinking of me now,*
> *Petitioning the Lord for me.*
>
> (From *Pencil Letter*; Hutchinson)

'A sudden sense of joy and warmth... someone is
thinking of me now – petitioning the Lord for me'. Irina
cannot *prove* that these things were answers to prayer
but we cannot doubt that they happened, for she is a
woman of deep integrity and honesty. So I would
gently press the question: what other explanation fits?

Some writers work on an even bigger canvas. Thomas
Merton became a Trappist monk and an influential
twentieth century Christian writer. When, as a rather
wild young man, he visited a monastery in the 1930s
he came to believe that prayer and worship are the
'glue' which holds the world together, and prevents the
forces of darkness and chaos from cracking it apart.
The Nazis were jackbooting their way across Europe:
what could prevent these dark powers from engulfing
our world? He concluded:

> '*This is the center of America. I had wondered what was*
> *keeping the country together, what has been keeping the*
> *universe from cracking in pieces and falling apart. It's*
> *places like this monastery – not only this one; there must*
> *be others.... This is the only real city in America – and it*
> *is by itself, in the wilderness. It is an axle around which*
> *the whole country blindly turns, and knows nothing*
> *about it. Gethsemani holds the country together: What*
> *right have I to be here?'*

'There was once a man who had three nasty big boils, and he went to the doctor and asked for each of them to be treated or removed. And the doctor said, "My dear fellow, I can do nothing permanent with these boils unless we get rid of the poison in your system which is causing them". So, too, the human race, very sick and having at least three terrible boils in the social and moral order, wants to be rid of them. But this human race does not grasp that the trouble is a poison in the system and the sickness is that of a deep derangement in the relation of mankind to the Creator. Go to the root. The root is the right relation of man to Creator: and when Christians are concerned about what they call worship they are concerned, not with something remote or escapist, but with the root of the world's predicament'.

(From *Introducing the Christian Faith* by Michael Ramsay, SCM).

QUESTIONS FOR GROUPS

Suggested Bible Reading: Matthew 7:7-12

1. Raise any points on the audio tape or in the booklet with which you strongly agree or disagree.

2. What do you make of Huckleberry Finn's point in this chapter?

3. How do you respond to Irina Ratushinskaya's poem, and the explanation she gives for her unexpected warmth?

4. Are Thomas Merton and Michael Ramsey overstating the value of prayer and worship, or are they saying something which is true and very profound?

5. Recent studies have suggested that faith, prayer, and worship are good for our health.

   (a) Why might this be?

   (b) Do you find that prayer and worship make you 'feel' better? In what ways?

6. How would you respond to a new believer who asked

   (a) how do you pray?

   (b) please help me to pray?

7. The best way to cope with doubt is to return to the 3 key facts in Session 1, and add to them the significance of prayer and worship outlined in this chapter. Do you agree?

8. The church is a mixed blessing. It often encourages and generates faith but sometimes damages faith and sows seeds of doubt. What do you make of this?

9. Read Matthew 6:9-13. What are the main elements in the Lord's Prayer and how do they relate to life in the twenty-first century?

10. Read Philippians 1:3-11. What can we learn from this lovely passage on prayer?

SESSION 5:
FAITH FUELLING ACTION

Some years ago I was in conversation with a man who was training for full-time Christian ministry. He had decided to stay on for an extra year at theological college, to take a degree. I knew that money was very short and that his decision would involve real sacrifice for him and his family. So I tried to dissuade him.

He rebuked me: 'Every Sunday we say the Creed, and affirm our faith in God as our Heavenly Father. Do I believe that or not? The only *real* way to tell is by my response when I am confronted with a difficult decision involving trust.'

I took the point. In the Bible, the 'father' of all faithful people is Abraham. When he heard the voice of God instructing him to move on to an unknown place, he responded by *action*. In an act of adventurous faith he took to the road (or rather to the desert).

In the New Testament we find the same emphasis. Hebrews 11 gives a long catalogue of mighty men and women of faith. Each of them proved their faith, not by reciting a creed (important as that is) but by acting as though God is real and active in our world. The Letter of James is devoted to making the same point. And as we saw in Chapter 2, St. Paul sums it up very sharply: 'Nothing matters but faith expressing itself through love.' (Galatians 5:6)

Putting all this together it is possible to sift 5 responses arising from faith.

1. Martyrdom

Throughout the centuries men and women have chosen to die rather than deny Christ. We tend to link martyrdom with the early Church. In fact, the twentieth century saw more Christian martyrs than all previous centuries added together. Famous among these are Dietrich Bonhoeffer, a Pastor in the German Confessing Church (one of the few German groups which consistently opposed Hitler) and Maximilian Kolbe.

Maximilian, a Polish Franciscan Friar and Priest, was imprisoned in the notorious concentration camp at

Auschwitz. Several prisoners were condemned to death by starvation, following an attempted escape. Maximilian volunteered to change places with one of the condemned prisoners – a married man with a family. The guards agreed and Maximilian was put in the starvation cell. He died on 14th August 1941 and was canonised on 14th August 1982.

2. Founding Caring Organisations

Many of the great social action organisations founded in recent years have Christian origins. Among these are the Samaritans, Shelter, Amnesty International, the Hospice Movement, CAFOD, Christian Aid, Tear Fund and Habitat for Humanity. They came about as a result of inspiration gained from the teaching and example of Jesus. They are the fruit of Christian faith.

3. Daily life

In the fourth century, the Roman Emperor Julian tried to replace Christianity with pagan deities. He failed, and in an honest letter, he explained why:

> '(Christian Faith) has been specially advanced through the loving service rendered to strangers, and through their care for the burial of the dead. It is a scandal that there is not a single Jew who is a beggar, and that the godless Galileans care not only for their own poor but for ours as well; while those who belong to us look in vain for the help that we should render them.'

Professor Robin Gill has undertaken research to see what difference Christian faith makes in the modern world. He discovered that the involvement of Church members in charities and voluntary organisations is very high. In this unspectacular, unassuming way, faith in Jesus Christ engages with modern society.

4. Peace of mind

The fruit of faith is not to be found in actions alone. St Paul writes about 'the peace of God which passes all understanding.' (Philippians 4:4). In a busy, noisy world this is a priceless gift. Few Christians experience it all the time, but most have some insight into this wonderful outcome of a life built on faith in Jesus Christ.

5. Evangelisation

The Swiss theologian Emil Brunner said that 'the Church exists by mission as a fire exists by burning'. Christianity is a missionary faith; the good news of Jesus Christ is for sharing.

This must not be done in a spirit of high-minded superiority, but with humility, love and patience. Faith in Jesus Christ was passed to us by previous generations. In turn we must pass it on. The torch of faith is always one generation from extinction.

True faith gives rise to loving actions and committed attitudes. It remains true that we are justified by faith, through the grace, love and forgiveness of the God and Father of our Lord Jesus Christ. Archbishop Desmond Tutu sums this up with typical enthusiasm.

> 'What a tremendous relief... to discover that we don't need to prove ourselves to God. That is what Jesus came to say, and for that he got killed.... The Good News is that God loves me long before I could have done anything to deserve it. He is like the father of the prodigal son, waiting anxiously for the return of his wayward son.... That is tremendous stuff – that is the Good News. Whilst we were yet sinners, says St. Paul, Christ died for us. God did not wait until we were die-able for – He could have waited until the cows come home.'
>
> (*Hope and Suffering* by Desmond Tutu, Collins)

QUESTIONS FOR GROUPS

Suggested Bible Reading: James 2:14-17

1. Raise any points on the audio tape or in the booklet with which you strongly agree or disagree.

2. Do Professor Robin Gill's findings ring true in your experience?

3. 'True faith is demonstrated, not by reciting a creed (important as this is) but by acting as though God is real and active in our world.' Do you agree?

4. From a practical point of view, most Christians are atheists in certain areas of life i.e. their faith makes little or no difference. Is this true or too harsh? How does it apply to *your* life – is your faith adventurous or timid?

5. (a) Do you have experience of any of the great caring organisations inspired by faith in Jesus Christ?

   (b) On the tape the participants give inspiring examples of faith in action. Can you do the same?

6. Does the large number of modern martyrs surprise you? Why are there so many? Do they have anything to teach us in our less turbulent lives?

7. Re-read the final section in this chapter ('Evangelisation'). Does your church have a concern and a strategy

   (a) for evangelism in your locality?

   (b) for the mission of the world-wide church?

   How can you improve your effectiveness? What do you feel about Ann Widdecombe's views on evangelism?

8. Could your study group reach out with the gospel? e.g. organise a supper or a 'wine and witness party' and invite friends and neighbours to join you in listening to an interesting person talk about 'My life and my faith', followed by discussion.

9. What do you make of Desmond Tutu's paragraph at the end of this chapter?

   (a) Do you share his 'tremendous relief'?

   (b) If you were asked to explain from personal experience how faith in God brings peace and serenity, how would you respond?

   (c) If a young person asked, 'What is the Gospel?' how would you respond?

10. Read Hebrews 12:1-3 and 13:1-3.

    Discuss these verses and/or meditate upon them.

Note: David Hope's description of his journey into faith is taken from *Finding Faith,* a twenty minute audio-tape designed as a 'give-away' (see centre pages for details).